DONUTS, DIAMONDS, AND DREAMS

BILL SEVERNS

ELECTRIC MOON PUBLISHING

Donuts, Diamonds, and Dreams © 2017 Bill Severns

Published through Electric Moon Publishing, LLC
An author-friendly publishing place.
www.emoonpublishing.com

eBook
ISBN-10: 1-943027-10-2
ISBN-13: 978-1-943027-10-1

Paperback
ISBN-10: 1-943027-11-0
ISBN-13: 978-1-943027-11-8

Cover Design: Mackenzie Fulmer, KCAI student/Electric Moon Publishing
            Creative Arts Department
Back Cover & Interior Design: Doug West, ZAQ Designs/Dust Jacket Press

THE HOLY BIBLE, NEW INTERNATIONAL VERSION®, NIV® Copyright © 1973, 1978, 1984, 2011 by Biblica, Inc.™ Used by permission. All rights reserved worldwide

Scripture taken from the NEW AMERICAN STANDARD BIBLE®, Copyright © 1960, 1962, 1963, 1968, 1971, 1972, 1973, 1975, 1977, 1995 by The Lockman Foundation. Used by permission.

Printed in the USA

www.emoonpublishing.com

DEDICATION

I dedicate this book to my family. And to all the families that love their kids, and encourage them to never quit, to try hard, and to follow their dreams.

This book is a practical tool to continue the engagement process with your family.

Children talk to your parents.

Parents talk to your children.

It's never too early.

——— ⚾ ———

ACKNOWLEDGMENTS AND THANKS!

When you have a dream, project, or a challenge that you would like to attempt to do, you start talking about it and hope someone will encourage you to move forward. It is such a great thing when someone offers to help and looks at you and says, "Hey, you have a great idea and I would love to help you!"

Well, this was certainly the case for me in the writing of Donuts, Diamonds, and Dreams.

Hector Casanova, my great friend, who is an Assistant Professor of the Illustrations Department of the Kansas City Art Institute asked me to tell my story to his students during a story-telling class. I'd speak, they'd listen and draw. Man, it was perfect! So, for a couple of years, I would show up at Hector's class and tell my story. The students would illustrate a portion of what they heard. This is how the book was developed and completed. Thank you, Hector, without you, this would not have happened.

Next, is Randy Williams, the Senior Director of Corporate Development of the Kansas City Art Institute. Randy provided a vehicle for this project to happen through his KCAI Sponsored Studio Partnership Program. With Randy's guidance, we were able to work together as business partners, students, and friends to make sure everything works for everyone.

Thank you, Randy, for your amazing leadership and guidance.

To wrap it up, as I mentioned earlier, it is important when people encourage you to move forward, and then it is really important when you meet the team that knows how to move you forward. Laree Lindburg and her amazing team at Electric Moon Publishing put everything together from A to Z.

With the various renditions, changes, pictures, inclusions, substitutions, thoughts, (complete and incomplete) rolling every day, (especially as we got close to the end), Laree held it together with the patience of a saint and continued to work to make this happen.

Thank you, Emoon, for the tremendous experience you have provided.

Like we say in the book a couple of times, your team-mates certainly make you better!

———— ⚾ ————

ENDORSEMENTS

"Reading Uncle Bill's book is awesome because donuts are like drinking soda pop for me. I guess it's kinda like… sometimes you have to give up something you like to get something you love." *– Brian, 14*

"This taught me how to go practice even though I didn't want to." *– Annie, 9*

"I enjoyed every word of *Donuts, Diamonds, and Dreams*. I will read it over and over again." *– Jackson, 12*

"This book was very different in the way that it made me want to learn how to have discipline in a job, and discipline to be able to stop a habit, like eating too many donuts. And I like the pictures!" *– Mason, 11*

"The book and the pictures are very inspiring to me. I can see now that I should never give up on my dreams." *– Luke, 11*

TABLE OF CONTENTS

A LETTER FROM DAVID, THE EDITOR

We hope you enjoy *Donuts, Diamonds, and Dreams.* We have had a great time over the past few years working on it.

When my grandfather (Da) asked me and my co-editor, Annie (my sister), to help him write a kid's book, we were thrilled to help.

I told him that in order for a kid's book to be fun to read, it had to have a few things: a story, theme, problem, choices, a solution and a moral at the end.

I think he understood pretty well what a "big kid's" book needs to have.

This is his story—my Da's. His goal all along has been to help you write your story.

As we finished the work, he asked me, "David, what is the moral to my story?"

"Well," I told him, "I think there are two morals to your story. The first is that no matter what happens and how rough the road gets, never give up on your dream." My Da had some tough times, but he never gave up.

"Next," I said, "we are all cut differently. No two people are alike. If people just realized that and were more understanding, the world would be a better place."

We have left space in the pages for you to write down your thoughts and dreams. It may be your first journal. You may be a writer someday. Who knows?

Remember, YOU are a diamond.
There is no one like you.

David, age 11

A NOTE FROM ANNIE, THE CO-EDITOR

I'm a dancer. My favorite activity is when I am in The Nutcracker at the Kauffman Center.

Da asked me what I loved the most about dancing. I told him, "Our performances every night and the way everyone claps and loves us."

He asked me to name the hardest part about dancing. I said, "The rehearsing every night and the number of times we have to do it over to get it right. It's exhausting!"

He asked me what I learn from dancing. I told him, "It may be a lot of work, it is really worth it. And when it is over, I miss it."

I love to dance.

Da said he loves to watch me dance. I really think that whatever I choose to do, he will love it.

Annie, age 9

MEET THE
ILLUSTRATORS

We are the artists of the Kansas City Art Institute and we hope you love our work. As you will see, we all love *Donuts, Diamonds, and Dreams!* Our challenge as a class was to listen to Billy tell his story, pick out a point that we loved the most and draw it for a grade.

It was amazing how each of us picked up something different and special from the story Billy told. Through the exercise, we learned that we are all diamonds and we all have amazing dreams. Likewise, as we had a few donuts together, we learned that we couldn't eat the whole bag. That would certainly hold us back!

As our Editor-in-Chief, David said, the artwork helps to envision what the text is talking about. They say every picture is worth a thousand words. Our pictures really helped make this book a shorter read. Hopefully each image can help you begin to imagine YOUR dream and what it may look like.

So, dream big; realize you are a diamond and get started on what you love to do.

Don't forget to enjoy a donut or two along the way, because everyone loves a treat!

FOREWORD

The day after my final football season ended in high school, I was sad.

I would no longer be playing a game I love, no longer playing every day with my friends, and no longer learning from the coaches I admired.

And I will never forget the day I cleaned out my football locker. The reason I will never forget that day is not because of how smelly my socks were or how I found my missing homework assignments. The reason I will never forget that day is that I didn't just go to school to clean out my locker.

After packing up my clothes, I hauled a dirty laundry bag up to our school's music room. I was officially trying out for the winter musical. This tryout meant singing and dancing (something I never did unless I was in the shower) in front of people I did not even know!

Other kids waiting to tryout looked at me funny, and I could hear a couple of them whisper things like, "He doesn't do theatre, he plays sports!" or "What is he doing here?"

I sang and danced in front of people that day for the first time, and they smiled and told me, "Good job!" Usually when someone said "good job" to me it was because I threw a ball or tackled someone to the ground.

Well, guess what? The next week I found out I got a part in the school musical.

I was going to play Gaston in *Beauty and the Beast!* And the funny thing was, I did not even know Gaston (I had not watched *Beauty and the Beast* since I was in diapers).

Yet, here I was, an eighteen-year-old high school senior venturing down a path I had never known. My parents were so surprised when I told them. They were almost crying tears of joy. And I knew it was because they were so happy I was trying something new.

Those three months preparing for the musical were three of the most fun months of my life. I would go straight from school to theatre practice, and I did not have to switch into any practice clothes.

The weekend of the play came, and I was so nervous before our first show. What if I forgot a line? What if I lost my voice? Even though I was nervous, I was also excited with a thrill I had never known before.

We did four shows, and I did not mess up - but even if I had I knew people would have supported me.

You know why?

Because I found a new activity I loved, I found new friends I never met before, and I found new teachers I could learn from and laugh with.

And most of all I had parents to hug me afterward and tell me they were proud of me. They were proud of me not because I got into the musical, and not because I liked to play sports.

They were proud of me because I was the happiest I had ever been in that moment.

So what new thing are you going to try? Will you try out for a musical like I did? Will you invent something to help others? Will you learn a new instrument? How about take a different class?

We all have a dream, and want to make that dream come true. If you only have one dream, I think you should have three, four, or maybe eight different dreams! Because you never know which new dream will lead you down a path you never thought you would travel.

Sincerely,
Will Severns
Husband, Son, Friend, Athlete . . . Gaston!

CHAPTER ONE

THE DREAM BEGINS...

Everybody has a story.

Everybody has a dream.

A dream of something they want to do, be, become, and achieve.

I bet you have a dream, too.

My name is Billy, and when I was growing up, I had a dream of playing in the big leagues. I'd watch Mickey Mantle and the New York Yankees on television and I would dream.

I wanted to be a New York Yankee. Actually, I wanted to be the next Mickey Mantle.

Artwork by Jaycie Womack

Watching the games on television was okay, but I wanted to play. When I thought about my future, I jumped ahead in time. I'd see myself as a player in the big leagues. I knew it would happen one day. I loved baseball because of players like Mickey Mantle. I couldn't wait until that day when my dream would come true.

Now that you know my dream, what's your dream? Go ahead, write in the book! You have my permission to use the space below.

_____

_____

_____

_____

_____

_____

_____

_____

_____

At the end of my sixth grade year of school, I had the opportunity to get a paper route. It sounded like a great gig, but a daunting task for an almost seventh grader. Every morning at 4:00 a.m., I would get out of bed, hop on my bicycle, and head out to get my papers.

I'd ride to the highway patrol station. Then I'd fold them with rubber bands, load them into my baskets, jump onto my bike, and peddle off into the neighborhoods to deliver them to my customers.

Artwork by Cooper Parish

I usually had about 120 papers to throw.

At first it was hard, but I quickly turned it into a game.

4

Although it technically was work, I created fun out of a tough job.

When you love what you are doing and are doing what you were born to do, it is not work. That is why everyone needs to follow his or her dream, not the dream of someone else.

Artwork by Nina Gookin

The radio dispatcher at the highway patrol station, where I folded my papers, was my friend, Charlie. He talked to the troopers who were out on the road. He kept them aware of problems and was like a big brother to me.

Charlie loved donuts and so did I.

He would say to me, "If you go to the store and get us donuts, I'll pay for them." What a great deal!

For years I would get up a little earlier than my usual 4:00

a.m., go get the donuts, eat with Charlie, throw my papers, and wait for the day to play. *We could not wait, Charlie and me, for my day in the big leagues. It would be a dream come true for both of us.*

Artwork by Cynthia Walpole

From the time I woke up until I hit the bed again, I had it all down to fifty-eight minutes, if the weather cooperated.

Weather was always a factor. Snow was bad, rain was worse. The powder of the snow was not as difficult as the wet of the rain. Once I started to move throwing 100+ papers, I was no longer cold.

With rain, everything got soaked. Wet paper is heavy! In the rain there is no room for error because if I missed the porch and the paper got wet, I'd be in trouble.

My dog Dyna and I had the road to ourselves. She was my long-legged dog who ran with me on my paper route. I'd whistle and there she would be. She was very fast.

I got so good at my paper route I could do it in my sleep and some mornings it felt like I still was asleep! What a fun time, though.

When the weather was perfect and I had baseball practice or a game that day, it was the best day of my life.

Artwork by Michelle Julmisse

As you can see, my paper route was a big part of my life when I was young. Here's what I learned or did…

- I got a lot of exercise,

- made a little money,

- developed an incredibly accurate throwing arm,

- learned how to please customers,

- acquired tremendously strong legs,

- developed responsibility,

- collected money—PHEW! You get the picture.

I made my work fun with my imagination.

Every porch became a base that had a runner heading to it. The paper had to beat the runner and be accurate. I could throw from my bike and hit nearly everything at which I aimed. And when I nailed it, I would pedal as fast as possible to the next house.

When I missed, I stopped, ran to get the paper and figured out why I missed—what was wrong with my throwing motion, or direction of the wind, or the angle of porch, whatever.

From daylight to dark, I threw stuff and bounced balls off garage doors, sidewalks, roofs, buildings, all the while looking for a game. You name it; I would play it.

I was working so I would be ready for my chance; dreaming big.

Do you like to dream big? You should!

When I had no one to play with, and chances were good I had bugged everyone I knew, I would make up a game in my head. Just like I did on my paper route, my imagination would be all I needed.

When the "game of the week" would come on the television, I didn't need a screen to watch. I could see what it really looked like all in my head.

There were no fields for playing baseball in our neighborhood. Usually, we had enough kids that I could structure something that looked like a team.

My friend and I would tweak the landscape to resemble a playing field, hopefully that looked like a diamond (baseball's played on a diamond, as we know).

We got the layout as close as we could, which worked fine because each of us knew what it was supposed to look like.

We played by the creek, on the street, on the parking lot, whatever space was available. Anything could be a base or a boundary. We called it our Sandlot.

From dawn to dusk we played endlessly, until our mothers called us home or the sun had set and we could not see our hands in front of our faces—whichever came first.

Artwork by August Demarea

My friends and I cheered for each other. We coached each other. We argued, debated plays and resolved issues. It was great.

All we had was each other, and we had to learn to get along so we could play every day.

Every morning, aside from school days, we would get up, have breakfast, and head outside to play.

In droves, we kids hit the streets. We were allowed to go to all of our friends' houses, but no early doorbell ringing, out of respect.

As soon as we were all in one group, away we would go to scout our location to play for the day.

Of course, I always lobbied for baseball. I think I usually won because I was the oldest, loudest, and for sure knew what I wanted to do. No indecision on my part.

Of course, we all had a say in what we were going to do that day, and if someone really wanted to hit the creek and play in the water—we did.

You have to do what everyone else wants to do occasionally or no one will do what you want to later. I learned to like all kinds of activities.

I learned that life was a lot more than baseball.

BEST FRIENDS FOREVER (BFF)

My soon-to-be best friend, Jimmy, lived far around the corner, so none of us kids who played at the Sandlot really knew him. He just seemed different because we didn't know him well enough yet.

Name a time you thought someone was 'different' until you got to know them better?

_____

_____

_____

_____

_____

_____

_____

_____

Well, one day, Jimmy rode his bike by our baseball game, and I said something to him. He stopped, and said something to me. I pushed him, and he hit me on the nose. I ran home crying.

Jimmy followed me to my house. He felt horrible. My mom asked Jimmy if he hit me and he said, "Yes." He told her I had pushed him and he just hit me and he felt bad. She said maybe he had better go home and tomorrow we could start over. We did, and to this day, even though we do not see each other in person very often, we are all still BFF's.

Best friends are never far away.

Artwork by Zachary Martin

Jimmy's dream was to be like Elvis. Therefore, many days, we sang. I loved to support my friend and his dream. We just loved Elvis. And Jimmy loved to sing—like me and baseball!

Jimmy knew his dream to sing when he was young, as I knew I wanted to play baseball. Jimmy had a cool dream.

Playing is about friendship and wanting your friends to have fun, too.

My younger brother, Bob, was quiet and went along with what the rest of us wanted to do. Bob's best friend, David, was not all that much into baseball, either. He and Bobby were great friends and both were flexible to play about anything we wanted.

Bob loved the world of mechanical gadgets. Bobby had a cool dream.

One day, he tried to fly a box off our roof. I offered to catch him if it didn't fly, but we never got to that point. Mom overheard the plan and put an end to it.

13

In the end, Bobby became an aerospace engineer. He has designed jets for the past forty years.

It is great when dreams come true.

do what you love the most

Artwork by Hannah Gibbs

Knowing what you love to do really happens early sometimes. I think that is what I learned from all my friends in the Sandlot. We all had dreams and, man, did we play.

Bottom line, behind every kid there is a dream, a natural ability and a heart that hopes to do something special.

What do you want to do that is special?

_____

_____

_____

_____

_____

_____

_____

_____

_____

_____

_____

_____

_____

_____

_____

_____

I didn't really care where I played, at what level I played, who I played with, how long we played or when we played.

I knew what I wanted to do when I was five years old.

What do you love to do? Tell me your dream again...

_____

_____

_____

_____

_____

_____

_____

_____

_____

_____

_____

_____

_____

In five years, I broke thirty-seven windows.

Sometimes I overthrew the porch, but I was accurate.

I certainly learned many lessons. I worked hard and filled my days and mornings with great imaginary games.

Because I had friends, like Jimmy and my brother Bob, I shared their dreams. Some days, I helped them get ready for what they loved to do.

That is what friends do.

Artwork by Clark Holiday

Behind every kid is a dream.

The hard work of the paper route eventually paved the way of working hard in other activities. Ultimately and maybe just as importantly, it paved the way for me to…

- learn the value of hard work,

- never quit,

- keep showing up,

- keep trying every day,

- learn how to be a good teammate and

- be a part of a great team.

MY FIRST SCHOOL TEAM

The big league dream got a little bigger when I became part of my school team, the MacArthur Bears. For the first time in my life, I didn't have to go talk everyone into playing at the Sandlot. Now, a dad did that for us.

The day I got my first uniform was the day I looked forward to all of my life. Finally, the day arrived—it was the best!

The school had sign-ups and all of a sudden, we had a real team. When they announced we were getting uniforms complete with our own hats, I thought I had died and gone to heaven.

When I was handed my uniform, the big league dream seemed closer. I didn't want to take my uniform off.

Artwork by Gabriela Pabon

Because we were now on a real team, we had real practices, real games and a schedule.

It was almost intolerable to wait for a real game. That is why the all-day-long games in the Sandlot were so important; the waiting time was shorter than a real game. When I was not on the field, a lot of my time was spent praying for it not to rain.

Unfortunately, the MacArthur Bears were not the best team. The MacArthur Bats had Randy Wilson. Randy was the toughest pitcher in the school, even on the planet, or so it seemed at the time. Maybe we beat him once or twice, but he was scary.

Who is the "Randy" in your life?

_____

_____

_____

_____

_____

_____

_____

_____

_____

Then there was the Hoover Hotshots. They were a bigwig bunch of guys. Their dads were super intense and seemed too involved. They usually beat everybody, but that is okay.

Artwork by Carson Kerns

When I got to high school, I could not wait for the baseball tryouts. My dream was getting closer. To be on a high school team would be unbelievable! I knew it was destined to happen.

I was a great ball player.

I was ready.

I had dreamed of taking it to the next level, and finally the day had come.

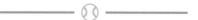

CHAPTER TWO

OH, NO! WE'VE GOT A PROBLEM

Now, I have to admit I was not ready in tenth grade for what I was up against trying out for high school baseball. My class had 808 kids and there were 110 boys trying out for the baseball team.

That didn't bother me.

Quite a few good baseball players showed up to compete for a spot on the high school team. It didn't really matter to me, though; I knew I was on the team. After all, I was the next Mickey Mantle.

I was fearless. Not a worry entered my mind. Tryouts were fantastic. I had a great day. I threw the ball great. I caught everything that came my way. I hit the ball square on the bat.

What a day; I was on my way!

At the end of tryouts, the coaches said to go to the gym the next day and check to see which field we would report to for practice.

The next day, I hurried to the gym. On the wall hung three lists. I checked out the first list. My name was not on it. I shrugged it off and saddled over to the second list. My name wasn't on that one either. So I sheepishly thought to myself, *Oh, well, alphabetical order. I must be on the third list.* I thought wrong.

My name was not on any list.

Artwork by Kaitlyn Jordan

I had been cut from the baseball team on the first day out.

Have you ever been cut from a team or been told you weren't good enough? Tell me about it.

_____

_____

_____

_____

_____

_____

Everything I had ever wanted had vanished—and I had only begun.

I was devastated.

Artwork by Lana Hughes

23

Jimmy had made the B team. At least he would get to play, and I was happy for him. My heart felt better as Jimmy told me he knew the coaches had made a mistake and I should have been on the team.

No matter how kind Jimmy was, though, I still had been cut from the baseball team.

I had been cut from my dream.

I stood staring at the lists of teams, frozen in shock. *I could not believe that the next Mickey Mantle had been cut— that I had been cut!*

My heart was in my throat. I strained my eyes to be sure I saw correctly. My arms and legs felt numb with heartbreak. If I blinked, tears would have rolled. And crying in front of the other guys would have been unacceptable.

I stood in a daze. Slowly, I turned and headed out of the locker room, sped up the stairs, ran out the doors to the parking lot… and blinked.

The crying came so hard I could hardly walk. The journey home was the longest mile I had ever experienced. It was all just too much.

I honestly believed the coaches had made a big mistake when they cut me from the team.

When I arrived home, I went straight to my room and had a few donuts to ease the pain.

HAD A FEW

TO EASE THE PAIN

Artwork by Shafer Brown

I knew my dad would come into my room to chat about what happened. On occasions when I had experienced a bad day, my dad would address me by a name other than my own, to try to make me smile.

It was definitely one of those bad days.

"Willy," Dad said, "you know you are a great baseball player. You have a great arm. You have very strong legs from riding your bike. You love the game, you are a hard worker, and you know everything about baseball. But buddy, it wouldn't hurt you to slow down on those donuts. They are holding you back."

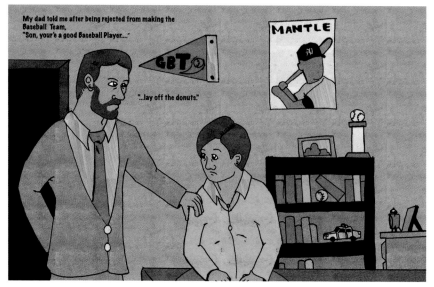

Artwork by Jose Leal

It was exactly what a dad should say to his disappointed child. He told me how good I was (a kid should always know his parents think he/she is the best), and then he gently told me the reason I had not made the team.

Now, I had a big choice: either I could take being cut from the team as a sign to quit or as a challenge to improve myself.

Do you know what I chose to do? I decided I would try harder and not give up on my dream of playing baseball.

I tossed the recent events around in my head like a game of catch.

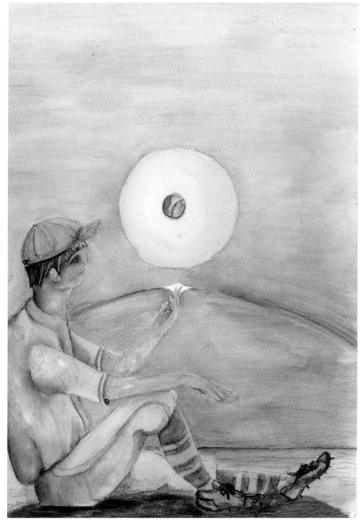

Artwork by Shelby Noel

How can I improve and get back on the team? What had I done wrong? I wondered. *Were donuts my problem? They are good not bad, right? At least they do not taste bad..."*

All of a sudden, as I heartbreakingly went over my performance the day before, I realized I had not run as fast as I thought I had.

Then I thought to myself, The donuts. *Oh, man—Dad is right! That was the problem!*

I had gained a bit of extra weight from eating donuts almost every morning with Charlie. I had gotten a little bit chubby. Those excess pounds made me run slower around the bases and on the field.

The coaches had not cut me because I didn't play well. It seemed to me that I had been overlooked for other reasons.

My next choice seemed simple: *Was I ready to slow down on eating donuts to make the baseball team?*

For me, the decision was easy. I knew I could and would do something about my problem.

Artwork by Victoria Khan

The donuts were holding me back, as my dad had said, and in a strange way, that was good news to me! I had figured out my problem and had already begun to form my solution.

My initial devastation of being cut from the baseball team had turned immediately to hope.

Getting cut, left out, and overlooked can make us tougher. Not making the high school baseball team in tenth grade made me tougher.

Now I had hope and I had to go get my dream back.

If you want something bad, you have to fight for it.

Artwork by Eli Harris

HERE COMES HOPE!

The high school coach asked to see me the next afternoon.

My coach said that the reason I had been cut was that none of the coaches had ever seen me before and there were too many other boys on the field.

He also said he realized I had not been aware of how many other boys were trying out and that I just needed to get in a little bit better shape. If I would keep playing, he thought I would have a great chance for making the team next year.

The donuts were holding me back.

GET RID OF WHAT'S HOLDING YOU BACK

Artwork by Codi Meier

Then he said something that I have held on to since that day.

"Your hard work got you noticed. I told the other coaches that day, 'I know we have to cut this little guy out there in the outfield, but he is chasing foul balls, and everything hit. This kid has more desire to play the game than anyone does out here and he is good. He is just going to get lost in the numbers this year.'"

My coach turned to me, "I wanted to talk to you and tell you not to quit."

Artwork by Jeffrey Schoenhofen

The real work was just about to begin.

My coach continued to give me encouragement, hope and direction toward what I needed to do.

Artwork by Jeffrey Schoenhofen

He finished by saying, "First of all, I am proud of you that you will accept this challenge. You are a wonderful baseball player. In addition, I am glad that your mom and dad let you come to see me by yourself. Only you can do this. This is your choice. They know they cannot do it for you. They are great parents."

Back then, I didn't have electronics or the Internet to solve my problems. I had friends, parents and other family members. Jimmy's encouragement was a big part of why

I didn't give up. My dad and my coaches helped me to see not all was lost when I had been cut from the team.

My life was full of people who believed in me. More importantly, I always had someone with whom I could talk. I think having a person or persons to confide in is very important.

Who do you talk to when you need to share your feelings?

_____

_____

_____

_____

_____

_____

_____

After my coach's pep talk, I was ready to go. A smile came back to my face. _I can always outwork the other players,_ I thought. _I won't quit. I'll keep working. Keep playing—if I really want it._

I believed that I could do anything I wanted if I worked hard and didn't quit.

Always believe in yourself. I had to step up, keep playing, get in better shape, then next year I could probably make the team.

Artwork by Jeffrey Schoenhofen

I knew what I had to do.

I WASTED NO TIME

The same day I had the conversation with the baseball coach, I told Charlie, the State Patrol radio dispatcher, that he was not going to need as much donut money as normal, because I was through with donuts. Well, not exactly, but I went from quite a few a day, to not as many, to ultimately not many at all.

I realized if I wanted to get to the big leagues, the game was now on.

Artwork by Greg Baker

I had to get rid of everything that was keeping me off that team. Therefore, I threw harder, peddled faster, ate fewer donuts and got myself in shape.

Once again, my dad showed compassion and came to the rescue by finding me another baseball team.

As I worked to get in better shape, I became quicker and suddenly I held the starting right fielder position. My speed increased and instincts quickened even more. My coach moved me to center field.

In no time, I began to see results from my efforts. I understood what was required.

My coach had given me hope. I knew the responsibility that lay before me: *work hard, do not give up.*

Do my best and play fearlessly.

Just as my family and friends had come through for me, I planned to do my best to come through for them.

ANOTHER CHANCE

That summer, the high school football coach asked me to be the manager of the football team. I accepted the position. Being among a team helped me get in the flow of athletics.

On Friday night at the high school football game, my friends and I were just hanging out at half time, having fun. The high school baseball coach saw me launch a football a good distance (thanks to paper tossing and baseball throwing).

The next year, I moved up to eleventh grade. When baseball season rolled around, it was a very different story than my tenth grade disappointment.

The high school coach called me in to talk to me, because he wanted to tell me personally how proud he was that I listened to him last year after I had been cut from the team. He was impressed that I had not given up, but believed in myself and held on to my dream.

Artwork by Meredith Lucius

"You can pick up your uniform tomorrow with the rest of the varsity," he said.

I had made the team!

My name was on the list!

I was grateful for another chance.

That first year, I made the All-City team. The next year, my senior year in high school, I made All-State.

When I threw the papers on my route, they had my name printed on the pages. That was awesome!

Yet, the most important thing was I was playing the game I loved. I knew they had made a mistake that first year, but I learned why it had happened.

Artwork by Brinnon Schaub

My problem had been resolved and I was so glad I had listened to my dad and made the choice to give up the donuts and work hard.

I didn't quit.

I never gave up on my dream.

I had wonderful support from my family and friends.

I took my second chance.

God gave me the desires of my heart.

Psalm 37:4,5 (NASB) says, "Delight yourself in the Lord; and He will give you the desires of your heart. Commit your way to the Lord, He will make your path straight."

And it all happened in the Sandlot.

I stored all of the lessons I'd learned in my heart. Little did I know where my hard work and passion for playing would take me after high school.

CHAPTER THREE

WE'RE ALL CUT DIFFERENTLY

I t takes a long time to grow up.

It took a long time for my baseball skills to develop.

I had to work hard.

Nothing came instantaneously.

Giving up donuts sure helped, but there was a lot of work to be done.

After all, it is not the big leagues right out of the chute.

Artwork by Allason Lewis

Artwork by Cameron Kunke

Baseball is competitive all the way through. From little league to professional baseball, most of us who competed against each other wound up playing together.

Do you remember when I talked about Randy Wilson? He was there on my high school team. We played together and ended up being successful teammates.

Unfortunately, we did lose the State Championship game our senior year, but we sure did have a good time.

COLLEGE AND THE PROS

After high school, I played baseball in college for the University of Oklahoma. During that time, we played in four consecutive College World Series in Omaha. That was a great accomplishment for our team and school. I also became an All-American. It was a great time.

After my junior year, I was actually drafted by the New York Yankees. Although I didn't sign with them, it was a cool feeling.

Instead, I went back to school and graduated from college and that was the best decision. Getting my college degree was something that I've always been very glad I did.

After that, I signed with the Milwaukee Brewers and played for nearly six years in their system. To me, it didn't really matter who I played for, I just wanted to play.

During that time, my dreams of playing professionally came true. I was never the greatest player of all time, but I sure did get to play. Until I suffered a terrible ankle injury. And that was the end of my career.

But I had no regrets because I had given it all I had.

Artwork by Miles Klos

That is all you can do

What did I do? I played **fearlessly**. You can't do anything when you are afraid.

Second of all, I played for **fun**. I always had fun. All my coaches made it fun. It has to be fun or it's not worth doing.

Because I played for great coaches, they gave me the **freedom** to play the game.

And I always had **faith**. You have to. I played for great coaches and people who had faith in me and in their coaching abilities. They helped me get the most out of my natural abilities. I think it's very important.

What are your natural abilities? What is fun for you?

_____

_____

_____

_____

_____

_____

_____

_____

_____

_____

_____

Like we said, it takes a long time to be great at anything. Whether you paint, play soccer, strum a guitar, dance or debate, there are so many activities to do in the world.

Not only does it take a long time to be great at anything, it sometimes takes a long time to even figure out what you like the most.

As a kid, you need to try as many of these fun activities as you can. You need to play them all.

What activities have you tried? Which ones do you enjoy?

_____

_____

_____

_____

_____

_____

_____

_____

_____

_____

It may take a while before you can really answer that. Lots of grown-ups still don't know what they want to be.

Just ask your parents what they want to be when they grow up?

_____

_____

_____

_____

_____

_____

_____

They will probably laugh, but they KNOW they are glad to have you!

It is one thing to have passion for something, and another to experience success at something.

SHAPING THE DIAMONDS

Passion, drive, success and accomplishments can come in any order. Let me explain.

In my childhood, passion for baseball came first. My love for playing the game moved me to work hard and not quit. (Remember, I had to make a choice after I got cut from my high school team). This effort resulted in success for me in baseball.

Just having passion for something does not automatically mean you will have success at it later.

Likewise, I had passion to play the violin. My success in that area was not as much as in baseball, but I still enjoyed making music.

So, we can experience success at something and maybe never have a real passion to develop it or it may develop later.

Once I had some success in baseball, violin and all the other things I loved to do, the passion for the activity grew.

But I still loved baseball the most.

You see, everybody is different.

That makes us kind of like *diamonds*, we are all unique.

Artwork by Rachel Doll

Once you have some success at something, and realize you are pretty good at it, it may make you feel like you are doing what you were born to do. It can take a while to figure this out.

That is why I always loved trying new things. In the Sandlot, we tried new activities because not everyone liked the same things.

Success or no success, it is important we show passion, love and drive for what we do and that we are fearless, have fun, play with freedom and display faith while doing it.

LIFE CAN BE TOUGH

Baseball is kind of a funny sport. If you hit .300, you are considered to be great.

However, did you know that it means you are only getting base hits 3 out of 10 times?

Baseball can be a very frustrating game. Life can be frustrating at times.

Nothing worthwhile is easy.

My good friend Ned Yost, the Manager of the World Champion Kansas City Royals loves to say, "The best way we learn is by making mistakes!" You can get better, you just have to learn from your mistakes and keep trying.

The point is that you cannot be perfect all the time.

You don't always win the prize.

Artwork by Eien Carpenter

But it is why you have to continue to practice, rehearse, and work hard on the things that are difficult. I call it "working on my weaknesses."

Everyone loves to do what they do well–that's easy! Practicing something that is hard is difficult. But if you don't work on your weaknesses, your opponent will figure them out and beat you. This is where you, as a diamond, are refined, re-shaped, and ultimately shine your brightest. So work hard!

The day after being cut from the high school team, I had to face the music. I had to either give up or figure out what my weaknesses were. Fortunately, I had an amazing coach who gently told me what I did well and how I could improve.

Artwork by Sarah Tennant

Great coaches and teachers do that. It is why they do what they do. They love seeing kids grow and succeed.

TEAMWORK

What made baseball good for me is that I was part of a team.

Teams are great. There is power in a team.

At school, in sports, clubs and extracurricular activities, it is always better when you are a part of a team.

Artwork by Penny Clarkson

Even in golf, or an individual sport, there is always a team behind you. Parents, coaches, sponsors; you have to depend on help. That is what I loved about baseball. I was a part of something bigger than me.

That is why I loved playing the violin and being a member of the orchestra. We traveled together, practiced together, made some great musical presentations and ultimately won a blue ribbon!

We pulled together to make it great.

Who do you depend on?

_____

_____

_____

_____

_____

_____

_____

_____

_____

_____

_____

Think of them and tell them how valuable they are to you.

It can be your parents, coaches, teachers, or friends. Just let them know how much you need them. They will love it.

Nobody can make it alone. I found this out for sure. There is a lot of hard work and sacrifice that goes into achieving a dream and the actual hard work has to be done by you.

Somewhere along the way, you will help someone or someone will help you. Trust me; they are out there probably helping you right now.

To me, sometimes a simple dream can be something that just passes through your head and then disappears. However, in this case, this is not the "dream" I am talking about.

PREPARE!

I visualized myself playing in the big leagues every day.

When I was not dreaming, I was preparing.

I worked hard toward my goals. I wanted to play. My coach knew this and encouraged me to work hard and never quit.

In doing so, he helped me prepare for the future.

The reason I loved watching Mickey Mantle play was because it helped me "envision" what I would look like when I made it. Great athletes, violinists, teachers, dancers—all have the ability to "visualize" themselves performing.

Artwork by Jo Stephenson

Find someone who does what you want to do and that will help. Artists have the ability to paint, draw, and show us what we are dreaming about. I would love to be a great artist, but I can't draw to save my life. Hey, we can't do it all, right?

Envision what you want to do, picture it. Then go do it!
I know you can.

PRACTICE MAKES PERMANENT

Back when I was using my paper route for preparing, my papers would land right where I wanted them to, and the imaginary runner was "out!" I would actually declare that as I rode off.

I could hear the paper hit right where I aimed. Remember, I broke 37 windows in 5 years, being a little too accurate, and flying it a little over the porch. But I knew I had a strong arm! That skill sure did not happen overnight.

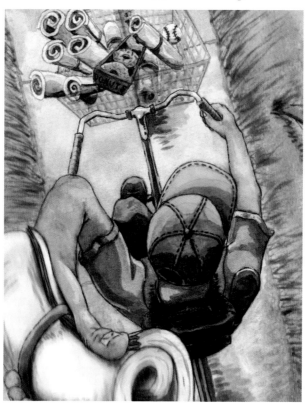

Artwork by Willow Hardman

I turned my dreams into reality with practice. Practice makes permanent. Windows were expensive. I had to learn to ease off the throw at times.

It is not easy to be great and it takes a long time to get great at anything.

Ned and I would talk about two things most of the time—playing fearlessly and developing our natural abilities. We all have something we do naturally.

Just enjoy developing your natural talents and you will do great.

Instead of loving to play baseball, maybe you love to fish, fix electronics, dance in the ballet, or climb a mountain peak. No two dreams are exactly alike because no two people are exactly alike. How awesome is that?

What are some of your natural abilities? Make a list. Share them with someone.

_____

_____

_____

_____

_____

_____

_____

CHAPTER FOUR

EVERY GOOD STORY HAS A MORAL, RIGHT?

My grandson David is my editor-in-chief for this book. Maybe you will want to be an editor someday. You never know. Maybe you will want to write a book? You never know.

Do you get what I'm saying? I thought so...

David inspired me to make sure I had a moral at the end of my book.

I asked him, "Well, what would you say is the moral to this story?"

"Well Da," said David, "actually, there are two morals. First, never give up on your dreams. Never quit...do not ever

Artwork by Brandon Hale

quit. And second, people should know that everybody is cut differently. That would be a great thing for everybody to understand."

David hit it right on the nose. My goal in writing this book is to encourage you to never give up on your dreams. Not only that, but to share your dreams. Share them with your parents, siblings, grandparents, friends, teachers, and coaches.

We all need support. When people know what we want to do, usually they can help.

So, what's the point of my story?

What do donuts, diamonds, and dreams have in common?

Well the ultimate moral of the story is this. Here it is…

You are a diamond.

We all have dreams.

We all love donuts. (Maybe just need to watch how many we love!).

Every *dream* is different.

Every *donut* is different.

Every *diamond* is different.

Wouldn't the world be a better place if we all just realized we are all different and that we are all diamonds?

We are unique and bring something "special" to the game.

You are special and made for something special, a diamond, uniquely cut to fill a one-of a-kind role in life.

So get busy and figure out what you love to do. Do what you love the most.

Get out there and taste everything. Find your dream and never give up.

And remember as my friend Brian says. "One day it's gonna click. It's all going to come together and you will be on your way.

"Work hard, be patient and play like your hair's on fire!"

Artwork by Joseph Maldonado

Now you have heard my story; ***what's your story?***
I can't wait to hear it!

_____

_____

_____

_____

_____

_____

_____

_____

_____

_____

_____

_____

_____

_____

_____

_____

_____

_____

_____

ABOUT BILL SEVERNS

Bill (Billy) Severns is a father, grandfather and coach—a guy who loves kids. His goal in writing this book was to encourage children and their parents to engage in a conversation about dreams, problems, choices and solutions.

As a sophomore, he was cut from the baseball team on the first day of practice. Seven years later he finished a college baseball career at the University of Oklahoma as the Sooners career leader in games played, hits, extra base hits, total bases, triples, stolen bases and runs scored.

He had to work hard, accept challenges and make choices to see his dream come true.

He hopes you will do the same.

Follow Billy's speaking engagements,
read his other books, and purchase his DVD
documentary by visiting
www.keepersofthesandlot.com

Parenting, Coaching, and Playing for Keeps!

Electric Moon Publishing, LLC is an author-friendly custom publishing place. EMoon collaborates with indie authors, ministries, organizations, and businesses in writing, editing, custom covers, specialty layouts, print, distribution, and marketing

Visit us at **www.emoonpublishing.com**
or contact us directly at
info@emoonpublishing.com